atlas of ordinary things

poems by

Melissa Butler

Finishing Line Press
Georgetown, Kentucky

atlas of ordinary things

ACKNOWLEDGMENTS

The author wishes to acknowledge the following journals in which some of
these poems appeared in earlier versions: *Carapace* ("Method for imagining,"
"Casting matters"); *Autumn Sky Press* ("Oblique"); *Voices in the Attic*
("8:13").

"How many times" first appeared, and "Method for imagining" and
"Oblique" are reprinted in *Difficult to Explain*, edited by Finuala Dowling.

Earlier versions of "This is why I trust glass blowers," "Of searching," "How
things are," "Imagine yourself as a fly" and "Millions of other places" are part
of the author's chapbook, *removing*, published in 2010 by Modjaji Press.

Publisher: Leah Maines
Editor: Christen Kincaid
Cover Art: Mario Rossero
Author Photo: Katie Long
Cover Design: Elizabeth Maines McCleavy

Printed in the USA on acid-free paper.
Order online: www.finishinglinepress.com
also available on amazon.com

Author inquiries and mail orders:
Finishing Line Press
P. O. Box 1626
Georgetown, Kentucky 40324
U. S. A.

Table of Contents

geographies

layer

collapse

inside

geometries

Acknowledgements

It would seem, then, that it is through their "immensity" that these two kinds of space—the space of intimacy and world space—blend.

-Gaston Bachelard, 1958, *The Poetics of Space*

geographies

The noon gun

The noon gun and the birds go—

they hold nothing of the day before
so I envy them;
not their flight or fear,
but the closeness of their world:

how it all happens,
and happens again.

This frame

The bird watches the slug
exposed on a soft, flat stone.
You watch the bird and I watch
you watching.

I hope you're there to protect the slug,
to lunge forward, snap the beak
of the bird when it makes a move.

You could ravage me,
if you wanted—

leaking what churns in me,
what I keep out of aperture—

plunge to my core, rip me out,
leave me open and raw, rough
un-fleshed and flat-out bare.

Oblique

They sit at an oak table rough around its curved edge. She asks him
what he's thinking. He mentions an egg and his lost red sock.
He butters a piece of rye bread. Hands it to her and asks her
what she's thinking. She licks butter from her lip and offers
a few details from her day: the little girl with a cut finger, forgetting
to feed the dog, wanting more time to paint. She hands the bitten
bread back to him. Tells him a small bird flew
into their window earlier. It didn't die, but was dazed.
He nods. Bends down to tie his brown shoelace and pauses
to notice the mole on her left ankle. He pushes it like a button
with his middle finger. She pulls her hair behind an ear and tells him
about the mushrooms she got for dinner: baby portabellos. He rises
from his chair to take the leg of lamb from the refrigerator. She says
something about rosemary. He presses play: *A Case of You* and sits again.
She pulls out one of the long hairs that now grow from his eyebrows.
He asks if she wants wine or gin. She gets up to open the metal cupboard
and removes the goblets her sister gave her. He takes the one
with the slight crack on its base. She tells him lemons are expensive again.
He removes his watch from his right wrist. Uncorks the '97 Cabernet
and pours her a glass first. They clink and say what they always say
when they toast. He gets up to make a phone call. She looks to the sky
and notices the moon is a faint sliver. He hands her a pen and she draws
a crescent on her left thumb. Later he will notice. He puts down the phone
and ties on his apron. She refills the peppermill while he chops onions.

How many times

She liked him for his details: how he folded his socks
and placed them in alternating colors in the second drawer,
how he only took baths on Wednesdays, how he ate
creamed corn from the can with a sugar spoon.

It wasn't that she didn't love him. She thought
she did. But on most days she found herself
observing him as field research.
She kept records of what tune
he hummed in the mornings, how many
pieces he sliced from a single carrot, when
he went out for the mail.

He often told her he had never met anyone so calm,
so accepting of who he was. She kept a tally
of how many times he said this.

Unraveling

The way things look soft from a distance—
a cluster of trees, piles of stone,

and how everything changes when we get close.

I sit on a piece of mountain,
trace my gaze along the line of sea below.
I need to believe I am held inside this frame.

When I was young, I thought
I could sit on clouds. Now I know
even what I touch will drift away.

Rainbows have no place, shadows
do not move, I will never get
to the depths of you, and

it all only goes away,

but even now I can see
my grandmother knitting,
the time her hands unraveled it all
because it wasn't what
she thought it should be,

all that yarn in a mound,
piled in loops below her chair,

waiting to be formed again.

This is why I trust glass blowers:

they know about the breaking.

(Remember): the familiar
gathers itself slowly
and then you are there, in a life edged
by dinner time, a garbage truck,
and the street lights
that go off and on.

And that day,
the one that made you feel
like nothing else mattered, the one
that made you say *everything*
is all right now, that day,
even that day is gone.

Casting matters

1.
If you're the kind of person who would worry
about what you missed after you jumped in,
then wormholes aren't for you.
You might be better suited for a house on a hillside
with a garden where earthworms work to turn your daily
egg shells, banana peels, and coffee grounds
into what will grow next year.

2.
There are few creatures as sensible and tidy
in the maintenance of our world than
these deliberate, underground workers.

They contract their muscles long, then short to move along,
to aerate and mix; they gurgle as they tunnel
their way through what we walk around.

A wormhole is a tunnel too, a hypothetical one
since the only way to go through
is if you're made of negative matter.

I imagine the symmetry of myself in empty space—
an invisible casting of my shape. I find my way into a worm's skin;
press my body against air, push it, stir
thick heavy layers, fold them in.

3.
The distance between where we are
and where a wormhole might take us
is no closer or farther than we are
to understanding what a worm knows.

A worm burrows in, casts what's there into what's new,
moves what's dark and deep into what matters.

You make me tea and there's a way

to come home. Like when
we stood arm-in-arm at the harbor
unwinding for each other
the lines of orange in the sky.

And later when our hands did not touch,
I thought of orange and made it mean
something it didn't. Once I went

walking to chase pieces of light.
As I got close, I found my grandmother
folding laundry, and me next
to the basket. Overlap is small
and the time goes.

I watch you peel an orange. You watch
the bits of juice spring out as you unravel
the rind. Your mouth, you moisten it.

She leaves her flat to walk,

to remember what she once knew
before he left
and she re-arranged her furniture
and bought a fish.
She thinks about her fish
as she walks. How he lives in water
but doesn't know it's there.
How he swims in small circles
and wants nothing.

layer

He begins his walk as usual,

around the block before turning left
onto Castle and following it
up the mountain
pausing only to record
(in the spiral notebook he keeps
in his left shirt pocket) the location
of feathers he sees on the street
and the occasional fragment
of sun caught
by a silver wrapper.

Overlap

That time
at the corner table
when he ripped
a piece of paper
from her notebook
without asking, drew
two overlapping
circles, pointed
to the part
in the middle
and asked her:
What is this?

she fell
into his question
the way other people
fall into love
and they began
a spiral of talk
about finite sets
and why
it's more than layers
the way
intersect plays
with merging
and how much it takes
to blur
the collapsing.

Tonal

It was a Monday. Early evening. She was wearing
her blue dress. She had been walking on the promenade
and just turned the corner by the Friendly Grocer.

She saw a man of at least eighty.
He looked as if he'd been carved from wood.
She stopped. He did not look at her,
but he began to say something, low and legato
that made her glimpse her grandfather:

The way he reeled the squeaky mower in the yard,
how he hummed in the mornings in the kitchen,
the day he looped that small fish off the rod
and he dropped it—flailing,
gasping, and wanting something else—
into the metal bucket it was her job to carry.

Of searching

And what of the frog who perches all day in the same spot.
Or the kettle that does not whistle. The crease
that will not remain flat. Or the bird
battling the wind.

And what of her reach across the table to take
what she needs. His eyes grazing the angle
of her neck. The faint music from her spoon
around the inside of her cup
that only he hears.

What of her dream. The slug on a wall
of faint shadow and slime. Her car
without wheels. The cupboard that empties itself
when she opens it. Shelves no longer
even with dust.

And what of the days with their rises and sets.
With their three o'clock appointments
and dinner guests. With buzzes to come in
and stop lights red.

Imagine yourself as a fly.

You see quickly
in multiple frames. Now grab
on to a piece of light. You go.
You go fast. You are traveling
fast and seeing fast.

And so everything
looks slow. So slow
it's as if nothing
is happening at all or maybe
it's like everything

has already happened.
But there you are, going on
and on like this. I wonder
what you're thinking. I wonder
what would matter to me

if I could see as fast as a fly
and travel at the speed of light. Maybe
I would think about how an elephant sees
the world or how it would feel to travel
at the pace of a new dung beetle.

What if this time

He said it was just what they needed.
And you can't find upholstery work like this anymore.
Side-by-side on the pastel blue couch he bought
at the antique shop on the corner.

She watches his hand stroke the fabric,
move his finger around one of the brass tacks holding
the cloth tight around its curved arm. She lights a cigarette,
reclines to stretch her legs over his. She wonders
how long he will stay this time.

He talks of the moon today. And Miles Davis.
Wants to play his records all day and night. She listens.
Wonders when his tone will change.

What if this time they sit all night
on this blue couch the color of the room
they painted that same summer;
what if this time he holds her the way
he did then?

She keeps her secrets in a pocket,

takes them out
every so often
to hold in her hand,
arrange them as cards
in a game of poker;
looks at them
one at a time
from top to bottom
before she selects which one
to play, which one to place
in the middle of a table.

It does not travel straight

Imagine a hole
on the other side, more

than a void; a tug
between heavy and what floats.

They only ever discussed set theory

It took him six months to realize he wasn't her tutor.
He carried the job description in his pocket for weeks
trying to find the nerve to go over it with her.
Neither of them ever mentioned it.

Her chair always next to the wall, his to the window,
her notebook in front of her, two pencils and a pen
to its left. He brought a different pile of books each time,
put them on the empty chair and only showed her
if necessary. She had peppermint tea followed by
a glass of red. He drank black coffee; two, sometimes
three. Once he ordered a bowl of mixed olives.

collapse

Chiroptera, hand to wing—

You taught me this one night.
You said: *Everything we see is already gone.*

The next day I looked it up. The moon
is just over a second old. The sun,

eight minutes old. Most stars so far gone
my mind can't grasp the time.

If time is an equation inside distance,
I wonder how far away you are.

Bats know where they are because they feel the distance
on the surface of their wings—

little bumps with tiny hairs let them coast the air,
skim the surface of water for a single drop.

They have an immediate life: send out sound,
read it, go that far—

again and again inside a framed space.

Sostenuto

She remembered the middle pedal,
the sostenuto, her grandfather had showed
her how to use when she was small

and so she pressed it there,
in her mind she pressed it down exactly in time
to when his finger brushed against her own,

faint and removing—
on and on like sound goes on
in another layer,

in its own tempo,
longer than it should, more
than seems possible—so

when they stood at the door inside that time
before there would be a kiss good-bye, a slight one
and off its mark and she played

with the ends of her scarf and he was talking
about how people think things when they say
something else and she hovered there

above it all to watch them both, oblique
and brimming-over and she looked at him
in small glimpses because that was all

she could take and after his finger moved
towards her own and she saw
his finger curl back and his hand go

to his pocket, she was still inside
that brief touch and they were still
standing there talking

about the lamb curry and maybe
the sunset or how there is more
than one shadow at a time.

A wooden plank rests

against a brick wall. They sit on it
as if it is a perfect bench. She peels
an orange in one spiral
of rind. Hands the flesh to him.
He removes a section and places it
in her palm. Then takes
a piece for himself.

8:13

A napkin folded with precision and left
on a table. The door unlocked. Two glasses
with last night's Shiraz etched upon their lips.
Music still plays. A butterfly floats
outside and a day has begun. There is sun.
Mail is being delivered. People are buying milk.
Inside there is only that music. It might
be skipping: a piece of a track echoing
itself in circles. She only hears her skin.
A pair of shoes is not in the closet.
A vase of daisies is on a dresser. There are some spots
on the bedroom window that can only be seen
with this particular slant of morning.
She can feel her toes. A dog barks.
That flutter may be one of wings.
She smells rosemary and lemon. A soft pillow.
A hooting car or the phone might be ringing.
Her chest rises and falls. There is something
slow or maybe heavy. Ten fingers. And a cat.
There is laundry to do.

Scene from a kitchen

She takes a slice of bread and places it in the toaster.
You watch. She walks to the window
where a moth is at rest on the ledge. She turns
back. You have not moved. She puts
the bread on a plate, cuts a piece of butter
and drops it in the middle of the bread. She knows
you are watching. You don't pretend.
There will be what comes next
and after that too. Soon
an empty plate. She walks away.
You are still there. You look
at the plate, but do not let yourself
count the crumbs. You wish you could.
You look at one crumb and trace back
the taste of butter. Your mouth
waters. It's not memory.

She eats popcorn

so she can trace
the scent later
from her fingers

to the scene
in the film
when the main character

walks from his door
down the steps
to the road that (although

full of cars and people
and dried leaves)
is empty.

Indexing

now

> nothing now; everything is all right now; something to
> hold right now; now it's all about mass production; what
> you know now; they are happening now; even now I can
> see; I can't hold you now; now drift; another layer of now;
> now grab on; that is both here now and was here then;
> that now grow from his eyebrows; it all makes sense now

table

> her reach across the table; at the corner table; your
> grandmother's table; and left on a table; they'll sit at their
> table; in the middle of a table; they sit at an oak table;
> taps his finger on the table; the corner table

hands

> something about her hands; to hold in her hands; hands
> the flesh to him; the time her hands unraveled it all;
> he hands her a pen; when our hands did not touch;
> never have they so much as touched hands; the hands
> that formed it; my grandmother's hands

bowl

> small bowl of salt on the stove; lift the bowl;
> a bowl of mixed olives; an empty bowl

cup

> she put the cup on the shelf; around the inside of her cup;
> cup the bowl; I choose to pick up this cup; maybe a small
> cup; my cup and the hands that formed it

loop

    it wasn't how his belt missed a loop; then makes two
    separate loops; piled in loops below her chair;
    no matter how many meanings we loop; stay with
    your lifts of loops and angles; the day he looped
    that small fish off the rod

keep

    its keeping; the body keeps living; they just keep spinning
    webs; it all keeps happening; they keep going on and on;
    it all keeps unraveling; he keeps in his left shirt pocket;
    turtle keeps on; it all keeps going around again; he keeps
    his secrets in a pocket; what I keep out of aperture

overlap

    two overlapping circles; two otters overlapping; overlap is
    small; overlap is more than what's there

piece

    a piece of paper; pulls the pieces together; just-ironed
    piece of linen; a piece of a track; turn each piece; takes
    a piece; on a piece of mountain; how many pieces he
    sliced; piece of apple; pieces of matter; want a piece of
    turtle; glimpses-pieces; cuts a piece of butter; piece of
    light; piece of rye bread; to chase pieces of light; piece of
    newsprint; a piece of geometry

memory

       and memory; traced each other as memory; maybe
       that is memory; from dream-memory; it's not memory;
       fragment of memory; what I trace to memory; memory
       as gravity

hold

       do not hold; the stories you hold; to hold right now;
       holds down; hold it; they hold nothing; holding of small
       things; of course you want to hold on; I can't hold you
       now; hold up the world; without holding time; to hold
       in his hand; lift that shell to hold it; the holding; I hide
       inside the hold; only hold things if; because I can hold it

matter

       like nothing else mattered; it doesn't matter, you know;
       it doesn't matter; doesn't seem to matter either way;
       pieces of matter pushed against other matter; no matter
       how many meanings; and this matters; into what matters;
       what matters to you

empty

       is empty; that chair is empty; an empty plate; myself in
       empty space; the empty chair; how they're empty; an
       empty bowl

distance

       inside distance; soft from a distance; you are distance; no
       distance; distance between where we are; and distance
       goes the other way too

lines

    there are lines we travel; drift some lines

space

    this space of edges; the negative space; a framed space;
    void-space-sky; edges of the space; land in a space; fraction
    of space; if they're in space; space of my thinking

time

    the very last time; outside of time; that time; dinner time;
    of before-time; collapse of time; how long he will stay
    this time; one-at-a-time; at the time; inside that time
    before; one at a time; this time suspended; distance is only
    time; how many times; this would be the last time;
    calendars of time; without holding time; one at a time; goes
    through time; have come to call time; more time to paint;
    and the time goes; different pile of books each time

inside

In that button

It was how he described the difference in geometries: drew a circle on a piece of newsprint, placed three dots inside, connected them to make a triangle, found the midpoints, their intersection, traced the length of diameter.

So I think about how I see a button, the groove inside its edge, how I trace it to learn about depth and round and where things go when they fall from where they've been.

Even if it's the thinnest possible button imaginable, it will never be a circle because I can hold it.

And the holes in the middle of the button, how they're empty, each of them with so much nothing—uncountable—and it's almost too much for me to take because if there's so much inside one tiny hole, then what am I to do about everything else?

It's the small things that reveal their perimeters and in the perimeter I find the between my cup and the hands that formed it, her glance out the window before she sees him. No difference between the curve of that button or the bend of his arm or what I trace to memory.

A kitchen, an empty bowl, two people, that same slight touch, there's never an end to the layers. I always find the same place in the same things—my grandmother's hands, a corner table, that button.

Kettle water burned my hand;

the pain makes me forget
my bruises from that night
we played rough on the wooden floor.
After you said you wanted to wrestle.
But that wasn't it.

I can't sip tea and write these things.
Even the fish laugh at me. (I can hear them.)

Someone once told me
I live in a romance movie.
But popcorn doesn't float once you eat it.

There's no map to show us a line
like where the sky meets the sea
or where the paved road turns to gravel.

Into

that summer we fell,
two otters overlapping

in each glide-by,
each graze of a whisker—

something
about you then,

how you held me
placid and hidden,

like that pool
(almost) a puddle

behind those rocks
in the sea.

Love affair

She watches him tie his shoelace,
how he takes each length
between forefinger and thumb,
overlaps one with the other,
makes two separate loops
(he does not call them bunny ears),
brings one over, under, through,
and ends with a gentle tug and the slight
turning up of the corners of his mouth.

He watches her peel the skin
off an onion, make a steady cut
down the middle, turn each piece
to rest on its flat side, make three
horizontal cuts sliding the knife
sideways into it. She follows
with vertical cuts the other way before
she turns each section ninety degrees
and dices quickly; she does not cry.

Remove

And memory;
how it pulls you in
to the places you call hunch or instinct
but what's there is only physical response
to some fragment of before-time
that for some reason remains
in your bones, in those places
you can't point to and say:
here, right here
is where I want the nothing,
the negative space of my life,
here is where I want
the emptiness.

Ways to end

That was it.
She swore she would never think of it again.
Nothing now but the sound of crickets.

It was the very last time it happened.
The call, the boat, that day.
Even the pigs wanted to leave.

She put the cup on the shelf and walked away.
Inside that room, he stood the way he did.
The only thing left was a small bowl of salt on the stove.

And the rain came.
She slept alone that night.
Neither the birds nor the moon had a clue.

How things are

Lift the bowl
from the bottom shelf
and hold it

in both hands. Cup
the bowl. Let your palms
feel its weight. Wonder

what has been held
inside it, what it knows
about liquids, solids, creamy,

or old. Listen:
your skin soft
against its curved edge. And you remember

your grandmother's table,
a just-ironed piece of linen over its surface.
You place your palms flat,

feel the warmth, touch
your grandmother, learn
something about her hands,

the way they work. And
this is how things are. The touch
and the years

and the wanting
something. You didn't know then
what you know now

and you don't know now
what you knew then. And this too

is how things are.

How I see the clouds

I am thinking about the sharks.
How I want to go out there and feel the bite.
Push through all that froth filmed with brown
and algae. The birds know.

Underneath it all, of course.

It's not like the measure of tides. The ones you ride out
and coast diagonally in. Always move at a diagonal.
When I learned this I was listening to the metaphor.
Maybe this is where I go wrong.

I am counting now. Clumps of kelp next to the froth. Wondering
if the sharks hide there underneath the surface. How they see
the shadows. The shape of things. How the surf boards
must flatten their view. Not like how I see the clouds.

The monks at the tea house spill sand for days,
then release their mandala to the wind.

Set of all things

Soon he will come to the kitchen and ask what he needs to do.
He will crush garlic and mint with salt and olive oil, then spoon it
over the lamb. They'll sit at their table and wonder what comes next.

She had liked him instantly. It wasn't how his belt missed a loop, it was how
he shared his idea at the party, like it was such an obvious thing—
the hidden worlds in the discarded objects from people's daily lives.

She loved the objects on his shelves more than he did.
When he wasn't in their study, she would take them out, one at a time,
to hold in her hands.

The day he described for her a broken button
in terms of its edge instead of its whole was the day she found
the title of her book: *atlas of ordinary things.*

They didn't get married; neither believed in such things.
She bought a house. They moved in. He built narrow wooden shelves
around the perimeter of their third floor.

They used to cue each other when they needed silence
(a blanket draped over either of their chairs). At some point
they stopped doing this, silence no longer something to notice.

Last week he put a note above his table. She read it. *Friday:*
cobbler, garden hose, press send. She knew better than to ask him.
Instead, she brought up a '95 Pinot Noir from the cellar
and wrote a list: *lamb, mushrooms, mint.*

geometries

She selects burnt orange

from the swatches displayed
on the antique tile counter
at which she stands on tip-toe
in order to meet the eyes
of the man
who has set out
this rainbow assortment of cloth
waiting for its place
to call home: around pillows,
on headboards of wood, over
cushions, against walls.

Method for imagining

Whatever you are doing, wherever you are, stop and notice:
the edges of the space, who you are inside it, what you can touch,
what you can't. Let this continue for as long as it takes you
to hover yourself inside your mind without holding time—
you are distance.
Now drift some lines between the colors or sounds around you,
let this happen in the rhythm of your breath so you become aware
of the shapes you make with your drifting. Let these breathe too
and they will make you think of things: people, scenes, other times.
Whenever your mind registers a meaning with an image, let it dissolve
back into a line (if this doesn't work, trace one of the lines on your palm
and pull as if it's a thread to unravel). You won't want to let everything go;
there will be things that tempt you to stay, but to linger is daydream.
Imagining is different. So stay with your lifts of loops and angles
until you get a sense of the texture of your thinking. It might evolve
as something you see or something you feel (or maybe something else),
but this is where you are inside the imagining. You will get glimpses;
pieces will connect without meaning and your ideas will seem
quite outside yourself. They will come to you because
you don't expect them and you aren't trying to form them.
This will not be romantic or spiritual in any way
because you are inside the immediacy of thinking
where such things don't exist. You release yourself
from dream-memory, let go of holding on
and something new happens.

Getting on

You can step over a shadow,
but you can't cut it away
unless you're in a Murakami novel.

I have unraveled you from my dreams
and taken up knitting.

Tomorrow I will buy a red truck
and drive north, following the line of sea.

And I will sit next to the sea
and learn to fish.

I will grow lemon trees,
knit scarves for my friends.

I will still have to pee, eat, sleep.

What Atlas knew of turtles

I do not know what Atlas knew of turtles.
But he stood on the back of one
when he was told to hold up the world.

I don't know how turtles swim the depths of sea
yet find their way back to the shore of their birth,
even if it happened a hundred years before.

I know turtle eggs hatch as female or male
depending on the temperature of the nest. I know only one
in every thousand hatchlings will survive to move on its way.

Turtles first arrived here 215 million years ago
and since then, I know they have found a way
to pull their heads back into their shells.

Air brings fire, fire needs water, water makes earth,
and there's a fifth—void-space-sky. I didn't know this until
I traced turtle's five central scutes down its carapace.

Many people want a piece of turtle: they use its plastron
for medicine, eat its flesh, turn parts into Crème de Tortuga
for their skin, pray to its form.

Turtle created the world: we belong here,
and "it's turtles all the way down"
quiets those who ask why.

Layering

My sister and I
used to suck jawbreakers for hours,
taking them out of our mouths to watch
the changing colors all the way to the center.

My mother prefers perennials
because they tell stories inside the soil,

and petals, how they loosen their place
from the inside—slowly,
one-at-a-time before they fall
away, drift on.

Sometimes I imagine sand back
to its shape. My mind pulls the pieces together,
a floating, but with suction—
moths circling in.

My skin can't release those years we had
when we wrote together, played cards all night,
traced each other as memory,
glimpsed each other old.

Butterflies are not romantic

I choose to pick up this cup. I choose
to take a bath. I choose to slice this onion.

But we are only bits of universe,
pulled along and torn apart and it all keeps happening

so of course you want to hold on—
his hand through your hair as he told you he'd stay,
your grandmother's locket when she placed it
in your palm, that taste of salt under
a Southern Cross sky and, the rain—how it frames your view.

But you can't bend theories for your own pocket;
patterns in chaos aren't there for you to coil
the cause and effect of your life.

You didn't meet her because you found a feather
earlier that day or because you remembered her voice
in a dream. To trace a line doesn't make it true.

How it happens

Before they watched two pigeons circling in the dirt
and he said *I want to be with you, I do,*

before they sat in silence and a squirrel
found a piece of apple, before he went on and on
about sacred geometry,

before they took the stairs from the fifth floor
after she put down her book she wasn't really reading,

before he came home from the store that day.

Millions of other places

When you lift a shell
from where it rests
on the sand, when
you lift that shell
to hold it for a moment,
even if you put it back
close to the place
where you found it, even
if you put it back
only a millimeter closer
to the equator or
the Southern Pole,
you nudge its release of sand
from what it otherwise would be,
what it would take from its tides—
and you become part of it,
tied to its imprint
because you bent over to lift it
from the place where you found it,
that place next to millions of other places
from where you now stand.

She leaves her brick house

with manicured lawn at five
each morning to run
with an urgency of being chased;
no one has ever chased her, but
in her loosening mind she sees bees,
packs of wild dogs, a choir of men
carrying scrolls and sometimes shadow.
When she returns home
she writes her lists.

Don't believe me

I say everything will return to sand.

I hide inside the hold of romance movies
or lists of what-to-do.

I am brave enough
to sit still and feel the breaking—

let it unravel
as more than a thought.

I am good at holding.

Acknowledgements

I wrote most of the poems in this book in 2009-2010 when living in South Africa, and revised and created this manuscript when back in the United States the following year. It then sat for a long time on a shelf. I am thankful for my friend Daniela Buccilli for telling me to take it off that shelf and submit it for publication. Many people supported me in the process of writing the poems in this book, including Martha Evans, Neo Muyango, Femi Terry, Kathryn Nurse, Tania van Schalkwyk, Liz Trew, Finuala Dowling, Colleen Higgs, among many others in South Africa. I am thankful for Hugh Hodge and the Off the Wall poetry group in Cape Town, where I met many friends and listened to many poems during the time when these poems were written. Back in the US, I am thankful for numerous teachers and writers at Carlow University's Mad Women in the Attic for supporting me in revision and continuation of my writing. I am also deeply thankful for my friends and colleagues with the Western PA Writing Project. Without the National Writing Project I do not think I would have found myself to be a writer. And finally, a special thank you goes to my dear friend, Mario Rossero, who created the cover art specifically for this book.

Melissa Butler is a writer, researcher, and educator with a focus on slowing down to notice and wonder. She holds an MEd in Curriculum Theory from Penn State University and an MA in Creative Writing from the University of Cape Town. She taught for 23 years in urban public schools. Her first book of poetry, *removing*, was published by Modjaji Books in 2010. In addition to poetry, she also writes children's picture books, essays, and other musings. She lives in Pittsburgh, PA in an old row house with a chaotic garden and a fluffy cat.

www.melissabutlerwrites.com

www.ingramcontent.com/pod-product-compliance
Lightning Source LLC
Chambersburg PA
CBHW021201090426
42740CB00008B/1179